Once Again Wings

by

Ward B. Welch

authorHOUSE

1663 LIBERTY DRIVE, SUITE 200
BLOOMINGTON, INDIANA 47403
(800) 839-8640
www.authorhouse.com

First published by AuthorHouse 04/28/04

ISBN: 1-4184-1292-9 (e)
ISBN: 1-4184-1293-7 (sc)

Library of Congress Control Number: 2004104928

Printed in the United States of America
Bloomington, Indiana

This book is printed on acid-free paper.

To Sarah C. ... May you never lose them again

Ti amo con tutto il mio cuore!

Table of Contents

<u>Black Widow</u>

"Don't say it...
Please don't...
If you corner a black widow
She'll bite," she said.

Relationships...
Whew!
What the hell am I doing?
I promised myself, "Never again"...

Consigned myself to the refuse-pile
Of failed romance...
Banished my heart and mind
From the warmth of celestial friendship...

It was all good.
Alone... at first... felt perfect.
I had grown cold to even the lust
For physical contact.

Then, just like the storybook goes...
Whamo!!!
Blind-sided by her glistening eyes...
And her even brighter mind and smile.

I have heard many people

Ward B. Welch

Speak of the instantaneous
Innate realization
Of "Love at first site."

Not once
Have I ever believed in it.
But this was something more...
More

Like love at first communication
Like love at first friendship
Like love at first understanding
It was more

"If it's not fair,
It's not time,"
She said.
I know she is right.

Time is not my enemy,
But my friend.
Time, friendship
And selflessness.

I have nothing but time...
My friendship is true.
Selflessness...
Well, I'm working on that one.

Caught in her sparkling web...
I do not struggle for freedom.
Wrapped in the winds
Of her being...

I hope...
I pray...
I wait...
For my Black Widow.

Ward B. Welch

Meditations

Lovely Lady,

I spent the day in heaven today
In my hopeful meditations
Of future moments spent with you
In love of God's creation.

The someday smile upon your face...
Your golden hair surrounding
Finally trusting eyes embraced
Agape love abounding.

Your warm and soft and gentle lips
Pressed sweetly on my cheek...
That thing we'd looked for for so long
No more we needed seek.

That unknown moment in oneday time
My heart did freely play
Again and again that precious second
I live to hear you say

I love you.
I love you,
Forever and a day.

Ward B. Welch

If There Is A Way

If there is a way...

> One single word spoken
> An action, a gesture
> That could melt your heart
> I will say it to you
> I will do it for you
> Never will I stop showing my love for you.

If there is a way...

> To break that wall of granite
> To free your precious heart
> For you to love again
> I will find it
> Stones crumbling to the earth
> Always mindful of the hurt that has gone
> before.

If there is a way...

> Of proving myself to you
> Of surely deserving your trust
> To alleviate all your doubts
> This thing will I seek
> Any sacrifice I will make
> For us to have that wonderful love that can be.

If there is a way...

> To keep you safe from harm
> From any heart's betrayal

Always cherished and respected
Embraced and cuddled in God-sent love
I will give it to you
This <u>promise</u> I give you, to hold you adored
forever.

If there is a way...

A week, a month, a year
Whatever time it takes
For you to want my heart
To see our lives as one
Happy inseparable loving friends...
It will be found...For your hand, one day will I
ask.

If there is a way...

Beautiful Sarah
You and I will walk that way together
Glad, content, glowing
Joyous and certain
Resting in the warmth of our love
Increasing to eternity.

<u>A Wish</u>

Soft
Gentle zephyr
Caress
My face

Warm
Easy rain
Massage
My mind

Sweet
Confident peace
Envelop
Me

Eternal
Lasting joy
I wish
To find

Ward B. Welch

Circle Of Stones

I made a circle of stones one day
In the forest, in a clearing still.
Walking through acres of southern hills,
Imagining my ancestor's way.

In olden days, in groves of wood
The Celts did stand and pray
To spirits of wind and fire and clay...
To the ghosts of water and wood.

I gathered my stones and brought them 'round,
Aligned with the old holy four.
The West, the East, the South, the North...
The Druidic vision was bound.

Standing my pillars and lintels there,
Completing that compass of old,
The voice of the ancient's stories told
Were echoing through the air.

I silently sat in that cool shady wood
Absorbing the sounds of the day.
Possessed by primordial shadows of fay...
One with my old ancient brood.

Ward B. Welch

Cold Autumn Evening

The sun drops below the distant horizon
Spraying lavender orange on cotton clouds
Colors constantly changing above one
The night descends, an inevitable shroud

A crisp wind cuts cool through rustling trees
Twisting whirlwinds of leaves across brown autumn
lawns
Anonymous cars glide quietly by me
On a gray-black roadway of chilling apathy

A coat wrapped tightly against cold echoes
Silently screaming surrounding my mind
Shivering and shuddering wind swept eyes do I close
The blackness this night like grist it does grind

Unlocking the door and turning the handle
Stepping into the house that mimics a home
Sitting down at the rolltop, lighting one single candle
Lamenting the honesty that keeps me alone

Long Time Coming

Long time coming
It's been a long time coming
So many twists and turns along the way
So much frustration and pain
Just surviving has been a miracle
I thank God that I'm still sane

I'd known the girl about four years
Always thought she was pretty cool
Couldn't give her much thought though
Circumstance did not allow
Still I knew she was something special
I hoped to be her friend somehow

Time went by and lessons learned
She found herself in her own special hell
Betrayed and broken by her one-time love
Her life once whole was torn apart
With nothing left but herself and child
Forced to make a bold new start

This is when I found her again
Right where I had been before
It felt so right to be with her
I was blessed to truly be her friend
One she'll never lose
No matter what comes of it in the end

I believe that we are meant to be
After all the healing is finally done
And life returns to her weary heart
I pray she'll then reciprocate
This honest unfathomable love from me
It's her sweet love upon which I wait

The day she finally takes my hand
And draws me to her gently
Bending my face to her lovely lips
Forever words my heart will hear
My love I'll give her freely
And always will, year after year

Once Again Wings

Once upon a miracle of God there was a woman
Who stole my heart and captured my mind...
Abducted my sight, so that I was blind
With affection for her, one of a kind.

As each day's sun rose and succumbed to the night
Our friendship was growing, of that I was sure...
Her soul-pained eyes had opened the door
To a life I thought I'd see nevermore.

I know that one day she'll heal and be whole
And to me she'll come, to be by my side...
No longer her love from me will she hide
Forgotten will be all the tears we have cried.

That angel-kissed moment in her own sweet time
When she from her freedom will gently alight
With once again wings; her love's crystal light
Shall envelop my life, and two shall be one with all of His
might.

Ward B. Welch

Working Mom

(For Karen)

You try so hard each day
To take care of your kids
Yourself, your life...
Hardly a thought for your own needs
Barely the time to even consider them

Day after day, week after week
Without fail, you go on...
Slaving away in blue-collar hell
Taken for granted every step of the way
Children who love you, but haven't a clue

The fact that you manage at all
Is a superhuman feat
With everything stacked against you
And the weight of the world
On your shoulders and back

You have more courage than I
That's for sure, pretty lady...
More strength and fortitude too
I stand in awe of you, truly
Not many could possibly do what you do

Ward B. Welch

<u>**Alone**</u>

Another night

Spent alone

In my house of silence

Beckoning me

          Downward

Into

The

Cold

Abyss

Lifeless photographs of joy

Stare back at me

Stunned by the

Solitude

completely surrounding

Ward B. Welch

Merry Meet

Hello she said, and smiled with magic eyes
That looked through me and caught me in such a way
Holding my gaze momentarily
Paralyzed with nothing to say.

Kneeling down, putting a coat on her little girl
A light breeze blowing bright blonde hair
Blessing her upturned face
I tried hard not to stare.

Beauty I had seen before many times
Never moving my soul so very completely
Unabashedly radiant her presence was
I approached as she rose up to meet me.

Hello I said, and smiled with adoring eyes
That looked to her longing for her love
Knowing in my mind and heart
She was truly sent me from above.

Ward B. Welch

First Kiss

Sitting down quietly by my side on the couch
Closer than she formerly permitted herself or I
Pleasantly surprised I am by this gesture
Of togetherness desired for what seemed forever

Slowly she lays her head, soft on my shoulder
Her hand reaching over to take hold of my own
Holding my breath and stunned by her sweetness
She'd kept herself distant for so long I'd lost hope

Enjoying the moment for what seemed like an instant
Hoping this joy would not come to an end
I couldn't see how it could get any better
Was I dreaming or was it just a twisted cruel joke?

Then she turned and looked up to my cheek
Her warm sweet breath so nice on my neck
Her lips then pressed softly and long on my face
Her hand turning my head and my lips to hers

A rushing and wonderful feeling so loving
Her lips on my own, trying and clinging
I melted into her beautiful visage yearning
And turned to hold her tightly to me

All time was forgotten in that celestial moment
Nothing else in the world existed but us
Finally pulling slightly away for an instant
She whispered to me a miracle that day

"I love you," she said.
"Thank you God," said I.

Chunky Butt

Sparkling little fairy imp
Sitting in my lap and squealing
Smiling wriggling flopping limp
Her heart's joy, my heart's healing

Silly tiny flitting fay
Floating all around the house
Turns her beaming face my way
Cuter than the cutest mouse

Shining little wonder girl
Grabs my cheeks and laughs at me
Plants a kiss just like a pearl
From the bottom of the sea

Little bitty pretty one
Laying there with her eyes shut
Gorgeous as the setting sun
Momma's little "Chunky Butt"

Ward B. Welch

Merci Beaucoup Messrs. Swedenborg et Vonnegut Jr.

Sometimes I wish words were alive...
That they could express the beauty
Of their total summation at once...
In a single collective moment in time

If the embryonic thought could be visible
Before the mind forced it into language...
If it could be physically seen, immediately absorbed...
A Tralfamadorian masterpiece, each one

Imagine that, if you will...
Imagine for a moment that each complex concept...
Each string of cognitions could be understood at once...
No linear trudging from beginning to middle to end

Totally illuminated, exquisite communication
The language of spirit and mind in tangible form
Pure human interaction with no misunderstanding
Perceived, seen, felt, ... heard with the soul in perfect light

Ward B. Welch

<u>Ashley</u>

It's a simple thing really
Which can enliven the heart
And you pretty lady
Have turned it into high art

You give it each day
To all who surround you
And to those lucky few
That you may run into

Everyone's got one...
As common as sandals
But compare theirs to yours;
They don't hold a candle

You can't really blame me
If I find an excuse
To walk by your desk
And try to induce

To cause and beguile
Or otherwise wile
You out of one more
Drop-dead gorgeous smile

Ward B. Welch

Runes

Runes of ancient times discerning
Future present paths to take
Love, protection, life wheel turning
Sound decisions so to make

Protect my love and give her courage
Give her joy in growth and change
Give her strength to fight the evil scourge
Wealth and power to her name

Olden symbols of my fathers
Thee we call to show the way
Love and fortune we shall gather
Unto us this very day

Ward B. Welch

Still

So cold...
So icy the steel
The excruciating pain
So exquisitely sharp and deep
As the blade is slowly thrust
And sharply...quickly turned

Me trying...
Trying to understand
The where and the why-for
How this could be happening
As the life blood gushes forth
Soaking and splattering the floor

I loved...
I loved too much
Cared too deeply
How can kindness be considered cruelty?
I don't deserve to be done like this
All I did was love

And still...
Still, as consciousness begins to darken
And slowly I slump to the floor
I turn up my eyes to you
Arms wide-open, lips quivering the words
I love you... still

Still

Thunder

When I hear the rolling thunder
I sometimes think of you...
What you've been through in your life,
What you're still going through...
The storms that sometimes fill your mind
From what's been done to you.

When I hear the rolling thunder
I sometimes think of you...
How you've come into my life
Like rain, then morning dew...
And when the sun comes up
To a sky of crystal blue.

When I hear the rolling thunder
I sometimes think of you...
What it could be like some velvet night
Alone in bed with you...
The crashing of the thunder
With a love so very true.

Ward B. Welch

The Flow

The spirit of Providence
A gentle current flowing
Pulling, kneading, softly under towing

To acquiesce I'm beginning
To its perfect intention
Unseen, needed, Divine intervention

I can't force my dreams
On that all-knowing wisdom
Leading, guiding, into His kingdom

But I can surely desire
That we strongly agree
Someday, unequivocally, you'll be with me

It's this hope I live for
That love's blossom soon grows
Twixt thee and me, within that sweet flow

Ward B. Welch

The Woods

Some things in this life
Will just never make sense
We'll just never grasp
A mystery so dense

What happens to us
As we stumble through
This forest of living
With hardly a clue

In the deep cloaking mist
That sometimes surrounds us
The woods close on in
Crushing darkness around us

Is it predestination
Which pounds us with loss
Or collective free will
The source of the chaos?

The most we can hope for
As we grope for the way
Is a true friend to love us
And give comfort those days

I'm here in this forest
You are not alone
If we help each other
We'll find our way home

Ward B. Welch

She

She seems so tough, so strong, so hard
This young woman so tempered by life...
Bravely facing day after day in the aftermath
Of complete relational meltdown...
For most, an unbearable strife.

I see her as so wonderfully independent
Consummately responsible and loving to her baby.
A mom, an employee, a student, an amazing
Lady whose spirit refuses to quit...
Refuses to give in to the devastation within.

She comes across as being so untouchable,
So unable to be manipulated, so intelligent...
I find it difficult to see and understand
Just how much these days have crushed her soul...
Pushed her to the very edge of the thin ice of sanity.

So enamored I am with her strength and heart
That I sometimes become blind to the woman within...
To the human within... pained, struggling, unsure, hurt...
With insecurities which we all possess and within which
We all hide, protect, and take refuge.

Dragon

There's a massive dark and powerful force
That embattles my very soul
Filling it with fear and doubt's due course
Possessing me part and whole

A great black-red dragon of old
Destroyer of life and love
Carrying with it death of all that's gold
And the slaughter of two white doves

This creature does vex me day and night
With cold insidious lies
Burning and twisting what I know is right
Relishing and laughing at my cries

Antediluvian Monster
Consort of Mara and Ba-al
The goodness within me does stir
To fight this serpent of hell

Nothing better would it love to see
Than myself giving up on her
The one angel created for me
This evil shall not deter

So I fight on, and on I fight
Wielding a double-edged sword
To slay that dragon in my life
And finally trust The Lord

Whats I Needs

Just hold me baby, hold me close
I need you so very much
To understand that I'm not perfect
Not in any way, shape, or such

I know I get on your nerves sometimes
You've told me so yourself
I know that I can be difficult at times
And think too much of myself

I need your help to understand
I need you to bear with me
I need <u>you</u> to have patience <u>too</u>
I need you to forgive me

Ward B. Welch

Runaway Angel

Kimberly
My heart goes out to you
I've been where you are now
I know it's not easy
But you'll be OK
It will all work out

I just met you today
Under the worst of conditions
So confused and unsure you are
So hurting inside are you
I don't know you, but I love you
Because I see myself in you

Things seem so hopeless right now
And your heart is hurting so badly
Misunderstood and unheard
All you want is acceptance
As the young woman you are
No longer a little girl

I have daughters myself
And I see them in you
You're as beautiful as they
And the world is in front of you
And it all can be yours

Ward B. Welch

Just have patience dear girl

In the mean time, I'm here
If you need a safe place
You have a home to live in
While you get on your feet
Just knock on my door
I'm here for you

To My Children

Brianna, Meghan, Jesse, & Anastasia
(Don't worry kids, I'll let you get back to your game in a sec.)

Dear children I have a few things to say
About growing up, about life, about love.
Sometimes it will all seem so very pointless,
But hear me my darlings, put your faith in above.

There will be many times that you just want to give up,
Throw in the towel, or just walk away.
You just can't run from your problems at all.
They follow you wherever you go, wherever you stay.

Never give up on your heart's precious dreams.
They are part of your soul, part of who you are.
Though you may find that you have to delay them,
Don't you dare let them die, reach for the stars.

When you love, give everything that you have.
Don't play games with the head, and never the heart.
Even when things appear totally hopeless,
Don't let love destroy you, trust God with your heart.

Now I won't make this long, much more could I say...
And believe me I will as the years go by.
Just remember don't ever give up on yourselves,
And as tough as things get, always trust the Most High.

Ward B. Welch

Dark Friend

So here we are
Finally we meet
The voice on the phone
With whom I speak

The sight with the sound
Alive and for real
To greet a new friend
Such a sweet deal

Mysterious woman
Temptation's daughter
You have intrigued me
With your semblance of slaughter

So my friend of the night
We meet on this day
With darkness and light
On our feet of clay

Ward B. Welch

<u>Too Much Truth</u>

I want to be alone with you
But don't want to be hurt

I want to be a friend to you
But not to be possessed

I want to be made love to
But not emotionally crushed

I want to give you pleasure
But not a broken heart

I want to be honest with you
But not your nerves to fray

But I believe that too much truth
Will make you go away

Alphabet Soup

You know I can't do that...
I can't just forget about you
If nothing else I must be true
For my own sake I must see it through
For my own heart, I'm loving you

So if the price I pay now
For my adoration of yourself
Is your unfortunate disdain
And the inevitable heartfelt pain
So be it... I'm not ashamed

Just
Abhor me, banish me, crush me
Destroy me
Eviscerate me, guillotine me, haunt me
Impede me
Jail me, kick me, malign me
Negate me
Outlaw me, perplex me, quarter me
Reject me
Scorn me, taunt me, unhinge me
Void me
Wrong me, "X" me, Yoke me and
Zap me

Oh, looks like I left one out
An important one I see
When you're through with all of these
Fill in the missing one please
Do me a favor, and just

Love me

Ward B. Welch

Let The Punishment Fit The Crime

I plead innocent your Honor
And beg the mercy of the court
I plead innocent of all charges your Honor
My fate to you I leave to sort

If I am guilty of anything dear jury
It is temporary lunacy due to love
I did not mean to make her hurry
Something slowly ordained from above

Myself I throw at your bench and gavel
And ask forgiveness for my crime
Please don't let this love unravel
Make it grow in its due time

The sentence you hand down to me
Should be proper in breadth and scope
Life without parole with she
Is all I truly hope

Ward B. Welch

The Sacrifice

"The selfishness must go" I prayed
"For the sake of my dear friend"
This woman I know needs caring and more
A true friend to the very end

A constant struggle has filled my days
A battle twixt old and new
The former clouding my mind with haze
The latter knows what to do

In order for me to love this girl
The way that she truly needs
A gentle friendship must unfurl
Compassionate in thought and deeds

You see she means the world to me
No matter my own desires
One day I hope she'll marry me
For now I must quench that fire

"The essence of love is sacrifice"
A wise man once did speak
In giving her space I do what's right
Her happiness is all I seek

I love you Sarah, I truly do
My dreams I'll put on hold
More than myself I care for you
More precious than fine gold

La Sicilia

Born in the fire of ancient trial
Cloaked in the cerements of kin
Spirit of vengeance as choking bile
Perpetuates millennia of sin

Land of beauty and romance unceasing
Country of mountain and sea
History of battle and strife releasing
Enmity 'twixt he and thee

Will this way of old not turn
To vapor dissipating?
Or shall it like the desert burn,
An endless conflagration?

Someday salvation will be near
One day this fury will be through
But 'till that day of peace is here...
Lu Sangu Lava Lu Sangu

Ward B. Welch

Sweet Myrrh

I'd seen that smile before
Seen those eyes, that face
I knew as I walked through the door
And stepped into the place

Oh my gawd was she fine!
Such a young and fresh little thing
Eyes dancing off mine
They almost seemed to sing

Was this girl flirting with me,
Or was it all in my mind?
Surely it just couldn't be
I must be double-blind

Well, I couldn't help myself
I flirted right back with her
Might as well indulge myself
With the glance of a young pretty girl

Of course I embarrassed her
As the youth in my heart was revived
But for her few moments of myrrh
I wouldn't have felt so alive

Summer Mourning

(For J.L.H.)

Walking slowly, sand between my toes
Morning disc glows over lapping surf
Early seagulls search the shore
Soaring semi-silent over shallow shoals

A light breeze blows off a glistening sea
Ruffled jacket mixes with hissing foam
Accented with the ring of a distant buoy
No one else on the beach I see

But the specter of a lovely young lady
Long ago lost to the land of the living
Lingering in the mist by the water's edge
Arms outstretched reaching out to me

Salt sea scent replaced with hers...
Memories old but not forgotten
Come flooding back, inundating
Echoes of love, my youth's first

I approach her as if under a spell
Her sad smile as beautiful as our last moments
All those many, many years ago
As she left for heaven, remained I in hell

Another step that mild summer morning
Her sweet soft spirit slowly floats back...
And as she fades into the mist
Once again I begin my day with mourning

Ward B. Welch

One Breath

Well, you win some, you lose some, huh...
That's the way it goes sometimes
You fall in love with someone
Bare your soul
Everything in your heart given freely to one
But yet you fail
Unreciprocated and unwanted
Your love lies bleeding on the alter of poor timing
With little hope, if any, of Venusian resuscitation
Where to go from here?
How do you let go of something so strong?
How do you find the answer to the one question
That has befuddled mankind since his first breath?
The question of...
Why?
You can't force the issue with Divinity
For it does not operate in something so humanly
manufactured as time
You can't force a heart to give back
What is given to itself in freedom
So what to do... what indeed...?
Take <u>one breath</u> after another
Wake up each morning and go to work
Come home each evening and go to sleep
Or try to
They say hope springs eternal
Sometimes that's all there is to hold onto
And when there's no longer even a hope...
There's always...always a prayer
If not today, if not tomorrow, then one day
One day... in or out of time...
I will find my <u>one true love</u>

Ward B. Welch

Kamikaze

Maybe I just need to go to sleep
I haven't done too much of that lately
A freight train of thoughts runs through my head
These days, my sanity is hard to keep

Today was a good day as my days go
Spent with my children in loving activity
I tried not to think of the girl on the hill
The end of Feb's fortnight would not let it go

We're friends, and for now that's all I can hope for
I'm trying to trust in Divinity's leading
It's hard when you want so much just to give
Receiving same seen on a far distant shore

I want to believe Kamikaze's behind me
Bringing my ship through perilous seas
Finally to rest in that much longed for harbor
Safely forever at anchor with she

Destination Of A Dream

Sometimes I don't understand
How we must be subjected
To so very much
So many times
To hardships uncounted which we withstand
And sadness so great with which we're affected

I take it one day at a time
Without you in my arms
Moment by moment
Second by second
I dream of a day when you'll be mine
Of your own free will to choose my charms

Since meeting you I have seen
A shadow of a plan
Hint of reason
Divine providing
Allowing us to go through all we've been
For the Lion to finally lay down with the Lamb

And now as we both begin
To do the things we need to do
Prayer sustaining
Growth maintaining
It will one day be worth each blow to the chin
If tomorrow and forever I'll be with you

Ward B. Welch

Hey Yo Babe!

(Forgive me Dr. Seuss)

One thing is for certain
Sarah my dear
I'm very persistent
That's perfectly clear

I can't give up on my dream
I won't let it go
You just have to see this
You just have to know

I love you my darling
No matter how long it takes
I'll wait for you baby
Just hurry up for God's sake!

P.S. I'll eat green eggs and ham with you anywhere! ☺

Ward B. Welch

<u>Hidden Hope</u>

As each moment passes
Of each day I breathe
I am keenly aware
It's you that I need

Regardless of all else
Which may come my way
I secretly hope
We're a family one day

Your sweet little girl
So precious to me
Is part of my life
And I hope I shall be

Her loving step-daddy
On whom she can count
Her mentor and friend
Who's love she won't doubt

And you my dear lady
From whom I must hide
My heart's true intentions
Locked up deep inside

If it's one day your will
If you'll have my life
You'll make me so happy
If you'll be my wife

Ward B. Welch

Shaddup-A-You-Face!

Hush and be quiet!
Leave me alone!
You plague me each evening
An impatient drone

Things will work out
Just shut up and be still
Have faith in Lord Jesus
And the perfection of God's will

This fear that you have
Immature in a way
Let the Lord bring her to you
Let the Lord have His say

This really can happen
It can my old friend
With God's love to bind you
You'll be one in the end

So hush and be quiet
Be patient, you'll see
That beautiful woman
Shall soon be with thee

E.H.S.

This is a test
This is a test of the Emergency Heartache System
This is only a test...

Insert two-tone generated sigh here
Sixty seconds and we'll be all clear
Yeah I know I ain't no Shakespeare
But I have ancient kin who rode with Revere
So like it or lump it I won't shed a tear
Oui madame, non madame, excuse' moi monsieur
But I love her with all of my heart, can't you hear?
And her love seems as distant as one whole light-year
My sadness is all between mild and severe
Sometimes I just want to fly to Kashmir
Stand there and laugh, poke fun at me, jeer
I know that I sound as nuts as King Lear
Hanging onto an ostrich flying over Cape Fear
All I know is I want her to call me her Dear
And choose me to love with a mind that is clear
And it sucks that that day is not anywhere near
So I'll just keep on hoping her heart God does steer
To marry and be with me year after year

This has been a test of the Emergency Heartache System
If this had been an actual emergency
I'd have drank half a bottle of Jack by now!
This concludes this test
Of the Emergency Heartache System...

Ward B. Welch

For Jill

Well my dear and tormented friend
The winds of fate have blown once again
And brought you to a familiar place
Loving this man; There is no disgrace

In your heart of hearts you always have
Wanted this love as burning needs salve
It never should have died to begin with
But life is so messy and often ironic

Maybe this time the respect will return
And bygones be bygones perhaps you'll both learn
To trust and to love unconditionally
This time for keeps, to eternity

For the sake of your heart, I hope it is so
Stifle our friendship this will, I do know
I hate that, but accept that, if happy you'll be
Your joy is what's truly important to me

So go and be happy my lovely friend, Jill
Forgive and forget and I'm sure you both will
But if, God forbid, eye to eye you can't see
My friendship's still here, and always will be

Ward B. Welch

<u>Inescapable</u>

Another twist in the road
A chapter in life's journal
Perfect in its inevitability
A stepchild who never strays too far
Change has once again kicked in the door

By now you're used to it
Though one never gets used to pain
Especially the pain of separation
From a dear, close, lifelong friend
And the lonely, empty hole left behind

You've been through this before
So have I, and if you're like me
You'll put up that emotional wall
And precious few will be privileged
To share in that private suffering

Well, you and I are friends
And in a short time we've become close as well
I've never had what you would call
A lifelong friend and confidant
But I believe you will be that to me

We'll never be able to flee from change
That very act precipitates it further!
And not all of it is negative anyway
Just know this my dear, beloved friend
No matter what changes come to us in the future

I'll be here to share them with you
I'm not going anywhere
Just call on me
And I'll be by your side

When You're Ready

I just want to give you so much
If you were only ready to receive

There's so much in my heart for you girl
If you were only ready to believe

I just want your life to heal
And I pray it does so soon

I love you so very deeply
I'd promise you the moon

I want to make you happy
I so want to make you smile

And I know that this is sappy
For your love I'd swim the Nile

So I'm here when you are ready
When you need me I'll be there

I'm waiting for you to truly love me
And my ring for you to wear

Time

Time is such a strange mesmerizing thing
Existing only as a construct of the earthly mind
Totally alien to the spiritual reality of life
It seemingly flows

Quickly for the joyous and happy
Slowly for the pained and anxious

If you are one of those fortunate enough
To have found that one person in creation
Born just for you
The interval between realization and actualization

Can happen so quickly as to spin your head
Or be almost unbearable in length and breadth

Time is simply spiritual distance
Between different states of mind or life
When the states of a man and woman
Sharing mutual affection intersects, and reflects the
other's

Then romance may be born
Then even eternity becomes a single moment

A moment... named

Now

Ward B. Welch

.

Dreams

He has dreams for me
He has dreams...
For me!

That thought just came to me
I've never looked at it that way
I don't know why not
Seems pretty obvious
To most believers
But to me? ... No... Not to me

Always the aberration
The dark horse, the outcast
My own worst enemy, of course

I asked a friend the other day
What is faith?
I've never known the answer
That single concept has escaped me all my life
A simple idea, don't you think?
But to me? ... No... Not to me

An empty word, hollow of substance
Void of any meaning that was tangible
Until this very day

Perhaps my failure to win my love
Was a requisite step in understanding
My relationship with God
What I must mean to Him
Even when nothing seems to work out
And my own heart's desires are dashed

When rock-bottom is hit
And all my dreams have died
Now I will remember

Ward B. Welch

He has dreams for me
He has dreams...
For me!

And His dreams come true

Meant To Be

I want the same thing you do
I need it just the same as you
Constant reassurance, constant validation
I want so much to give it to you
And so much to receive it from you

While I try each day and night
To keep my heart in check
To let you go and heal
Your mind and heart and soul
So someday you'll be whole

I still can't help but love you
I still can't cease from wanting
From needing, from adoring you profoundly
I have to believe one day you'll be mine
And that you'll love me in all due time

I have no other choice, my love
I'm sure to my deepest innermost core
That you're the only woman for me
So I wait for that celestial day
Though it may never come my way

Yes, I'm aware of that possibility
In all likelihood a distinct probability
But never again will I settle for less for myself
Than that one precious lady meant for me
For I've been succinctly told, we are meant to be

Ward B. Welch

I Don't Care

I don't care if you're poison
I don't care if you kill me
I don't care now what happens
I love you
I love you

I don't care if you're poison
I don't care if you're scared of me
I don't care if you can't handle me
I love you
I love you

I don't care if you're poison
I don't care if you want someone else
I don't care if I'm a complete fool
I love you
I love you

I don't care if you're poison
I don't care if your friends hate me
I don't care if your mom hates me
I love you
I love you

I don't care if you're poison
I don't care if you kill me
I know you have the antidote
Just love me
Just love me

Ward B. Welch

<u>Haunted</u>

It must be my imagination
That keeps playing tricks on me
Strange things appear to be happening
In my small-town Alabama home
I swear to you things keep moving
And that here, I'm not alone

I walk out of the room
Just for a moment or two
When I return, something's changed
Something's a bit out of place
Yes I'm aware that sounds crazy
And I can see the look on your face

If this had only happened
One time or maybe two
I'd completely agree with you
And discount the whole possibility
But it has happened too many times
To not become a probability

Things in my house move
Mostly in the living room and kitchen
They don't move very far
Just enough to catch my eye
And send an uneasy chill down my spine

Ward B. Welch
Believe me, this is no lie

I put the things back in their place
Every time I see they've moved
And minutes later, sometimes hours
They move again, without my seeing
I try to ignore it as best I can
But it shakes me to the core of my being

I've lived with this for two years now
And pretended that its just my cats
Thinking that they're the ones
Who've moved my things from where they sit
Most of it they can't reach if they wanted to
For them, too heavy to move a bit

I suppose I just need to get used to it
And welcome these mischievous spirits in
To my house and home and everyday life
And try to remain undaunted
While I live in this house
That I fear is haunted

Kiss Away Your Tears

Of all the times we've spent together
Enjoying the company
The one I like to remember most
Is the time you needed me

To rub your back, your neck and shoulders
While you were laying there...
It was so nice to dote on you
To lovingly give you care.

The pleasured look upon your face,
Softly breathing with closed eyes...
Let me know with each deep squeeze
Much appreciated then was I.

The feelings that welled up in me
So strong, so powerful...
My chest just wanted to explode...
My heart so very full.

If each and every single day...
If you'd only let me Dear...
I'd give you all I had to give,
And kiss away your tears.

Ward B. Welch

Pearl Of Great Price

Can it be...is it real this time?
I never really though it would ever happen to me
Never really believed it could
I've just been through too much in my life
Too many failures in the realm of the heart
I'd lost all faith in humankind

It used to be when I was young
That true ideal had a firm grip on my mind
Blindly expected it to magically manifest
I'd had so much drilled into my brain
Of the heavenly conjugial nuptial state
And angelic marriage bells to be wrung

Still here she was just standing there
A soul who had come quickly to be my friend
A tarnished angel of earthly light
Who's past lives so succinctly reflected my own
Struggling to find an answer within
And a need to once again learn how to care

I soon realized I'd lost grip of my heart
Something I never planned on allowing again
I saw in this lady a beauty unknown
In my world or any other I knew
I'd set out to sell all my proprial wares
For my Pearl of Great Price, so forever could start

Ward B. Welch

It's All Good

It's all good Babe
For real
No kidding
No mas Chiquita
I know the deal

It won't be to me
I know
I'm sure
It won't be to me
Your love does flow

But it's all all right
O.K.
No problem
I'm certain you'll find
Your man one day

When you find him
I'll sigh
I'll smile
May he love you
Half as much as I

Random Realities?

We want redemption in the arms of a lover
We want redemption in the eyes of another
We want redemption and something to cover
The sins of the lives we've all lived

It's true that romance and life take their toll
It's true that we all need much to be whole
It's true that these things are beyond our control
No matter how hard we all struggle

Sometimes it seems there's no decent answer
Sometimes it seems the world's full of cancer
Sometimes it seems we're all awkward dancers
In fate's heartless stage production

The day will come when I'm not alone
The day will come when your heart is not stone
The day will come when we both will have thrown
Away caution and fear, and taken a chance

I'm not giving up on joyous elation
I'm not giving up on my errant salvation
I'm not giving up on God's awesome creation
That He made when He realized you

Ward B. Welch

Please Don't

Please don't go back to him.
Please find it in your heart to love me.
I know you have a history with him,
But with you is where I wish to be.

I can't compete with old memories
That have become better with passage of time.
I don't stand a chance against that please.
And I love you with heart and mind.

If you would only give me a chance
To show you my love is real.
Just once before running to dance
With the man whom my fate will seal.

I beg you my dear lovely girl...
You've been there, you've done that before.
Please Darling give my heart a whirl
And be happy forevermore.

<u>Siren's Song</u>

(Die to Live)

"A patient man need stand firm but for a time,
and then contentment comes back to him.
For a while he holds back his words, then
The lips of many herald his wisdom."
Sirach 1, 20 & 21

**The strength of the ages had forsaken me
Or rather I had forsaken it.
Giving myself to my own machinations,
Sending myself to the pit.**

**The sly and cunning siren of old
Had once again captured my mind.
Imprisoning me on an island of rock,
No peace there could I find.**

**Anxious anxiety ruled my days.
Melancholia devoured the night.
The one whom I loved I was forcing away.
Heaven was fading from sight.**

I cried out to God and the angels above.

I knew that in order to live,
Myself I must sacrifice here and now,
And trust be willing to give.

A smile stole across my face right then.
The prison bars crumbling to dirt.
Slowly moving away from them,
And my self-made world of hurt.

Down to the edge of the island shore,
Carefully finding my way...
Boarding the ship that shall take me to
thee,
And true happiness some sunny day.

"A good wife is a generous gift
bestowed upon him who fears
The Lord."

Sirach 26, 3

Someday Sarah

Someday Sarah
You'll make it through this time
You'll smile every day
I promise to try to find a way
Each and every day to make you happy

Someday Sarah
You'll lay in your bed at night
Holding your pillow tight
Whispering my name into the darkness
Longing for me to be there

Someday Sarah
You'll call me to your side
Into my hands yours will slide
Pulling me to you, you'll look up
And kiss me long and tenderly

Someday Sarah
We'll be on a romantic date
Glowing candles by our plates
And me on one knee looking up at your pretty face
Begging you, with me to spend eternity

Someday Sarah
Ten thousand years ahead
When all is done and said
You'll rest your lovely head in my lap
Our forever will have barely begun

Ward B. Welch

That Time Of Year

Springtime...
A time for fresh zephyrs of warmth
When the world renews itself with life
When every lover finds new inspiration
And hope for the future is easier to hold onto

Springtime...
Above all other seasons, fills the mind with joy
Hearts overflowing with born-again expectation
Positivity becoming an irresistible flowing current
But for me, nothing...nothing of the sort

Springtime...
And the woman I love with all my heart
The woman whose priceless presence has entered my life
This beautiful world-wearied spirit
Alas, she does not want that love from me

Springtime...
And while the rest of the universe revels in light
And the color returns to both land and sky
The gentle cradle of God's loving arms embraces all
Save one... left behind... in love, alone... am I

Photograph

Faded colors edges curled around
A vision of joy never forgotten...
Cracked and fragile smiles bring back
The birth of a love unceasingly true.

Gently layers of decades dust removed
Revealing the confidence of easy hearts...
Yellowed paper image held close to view
With cherished eyes who's fire time cannot erase.

Rolling down a wrinkled cheek descending
Silently through incensed air...
A single happy ancient tear is caught
And shared by two whom love has made one.

Ward B. Welch

<u>Teacher</u>

There's a time for everything
In this life of ours.
Most especially a time for
Understanding and compassion,
Caring and selflessness,
Resignation to sacrifice.

Each and every one of us
Must travel our own
Sovereign path to God, which
No religion can guide,
No dogma can satisfy,
No human philosophy can quench.

You, my dear lady
Have in mere months
Aided me in my journey immeasurably...
Opened my eyes to myself...
Taught me to love by letting go...
Offered truly forgiving friendship.

If (God forbid) I never see you again,
I have gained so very much
From knowing you such a short time.
My life is more abundantly full of meaning...
Full of gentle optimism...

Full of joy and hope for the future.

You, my dear lady
Who still has so much to learn...
Are teaching me how
To live.

The Real Thing

I'll never stop believing in the real thing
I'll never give up hoping for that perfection
I can never turn my back on the promise
That's been given to all true human beings

Like all those who truly long for that miracle,
I long for it, and like many before me,
I fall short of deserving that blessing
And still, I refuse to give up on it

"Ask whatever you want, believing, and it shall be given"
Isn't that what the Big Guy says?
He means it, doesn't he? Sure he does.
So I'll never stop believing in the real thing

If I have saint-like patience
If I can hold onto what little faith I have
If God still performs miracles today
He'll give me the real thing... He'll give me you.

Vision In The Wind

It's coming, isn't it?
The wind is blowing
Clouds fast across a bright
Struggling moon...
You... sitting on the outside rocker
Listening... watching... absorbing...

Releasing all thought
Finding your center
A center which has long alluded you...
It's there though
You may not see it now
But it is, and you'll find it

Another large and strong gust
The trees lean and strain
I'm here too
Though you probably haven't noticed
I see you in the moon's infrequent light
And wish we were together

Sitting silently with each other
One in spirit with the wind
Taking in the oncoming storm
Breathing and existing in unison
Innately acknowledging the miraculous reality
Of two who've become one

The Rightness Of Us

I saw your face today... beaming and bright!
As I was playing so joyfully with your daughter
Taking pleasure in the glee she was feeling
While we cavorted and laughed

You were happy... truly happy
As she and I enjoyed those moments
Lovingly frolicking on the lawn
The joy on your face was obvious and welcome

Perhaps in your secret heart
You saw how it could be with us
If we were a family together
As one day it could be if you so desired

Well, I don't mean to misinterpret
The reality of what I thought I saw
This afternoon on your front yard and lawn
Those precious moments, when we were like a real
family

Yes, I do dream of that scenario with you and she
I can't help but see that lovely possibility
It would be so very perfect if it came to be
The truth of that does scare you these days, I know

But Darling, the true meaning of life is there
I just know you must see that in your life
With all the travail and concern for your future
Deep down inside, you know what is truly important

You know that above money and career
That what is really valuable in life is love
Not just true love between a man and a woman
But true familial love together as a complete whole

We have what it takes dear woman
We really do... that truth is what keeps you distant
For these days you simply cannot allow it
You can't permit yourself to take that chance

Understand that fact, I most surely do
And though you may not believe me at all,
Considering my blatantly professed adoration...
I do support your personal ambition and desires

Lady, I'd vote for you for President
I'd elect you to the Papacy in Rome
I'd buy you the one-way ticket to your future
Even if it meant I'd never see you again

I've been without you all my life
Do you think I couldn't make the remainder
Without you in my arms and by my side?
Of course I could... God forbid it! But, I could

I'm here for you when and if you want me
When and if you finally want the real thing
When and if love...agape love... becomes a priority
When you finally realize the rightness of <u>us</u>

The Tragedy Of A Certain Irrefutable Reality

Unrequited love
The connotations and implications
Of those two simple words...
Fourteen letters of desperate pleading sorrow
Press down on me like a black lead shawl

No other sad circumstance
Can equally generate such a plethora
Of soul-crushing emotions
Of self immolations
As the irrefutable reality of a love unreciprocated

The strongest of spirits
Lay prostrate...sapped of all delight
When its heart is happily offered
With great loving expectation and anticipation
Only to be unceremoniously spurned

It tries to maintain a residuum of hope
Seeks any small sign from its beloved
The tiniest crumb of returned affection
The life-giving breath of a momentary glance
Anything at all to cling to which will sustain it

As hopeless as it may appear
Even when all rationality dictates the obvious
And the fine line between love and obsession
Disappears in the mists of pure yearning...

Ward B. Welch

I remain your fool...I remain your humble servant

I remain deeply and completely
In love with
You

About The Author

Ward Welch grew up in Willow Grove and Bryn Athyn PA, suburbs of Philadelphia. After a three year enlistment in the Army, where he served as a member of the 14th Army Band at Fort McClellan, Alabama, he attended Jacksonville State University, graduating with a BA in Mass Communication. During his university days and for over a decade after finishing his studies, Ward worked as a radio announcer at numerous stations in N.E. Alabama and West Georgia using an old high school nickname "Woody." For the past nine years he has worked as a real estate appraiser for Calhoun County, Alabama.

www.ingramcontent.com/pod-product-compliance
Lightning Source LLC
Chambersburg PA
CBHW051427280526
45785CB00003B/1188